Su1

Start With Why

How Great Leaders Inspire Everyone to Take Action

by Simon Sinek

Instaread

Please Note

This is a summary with analysis.

Copyright © 2016 by Instaread. All rights reserved worldwide. No part of this publication may be reproduced or transmitted in any form without the prior written consent of the publisher.

Limit of Liability/Disclaimer of Warranty: The publisher and author make no representations or warranties with respect to the accuracy or completeness of these contents and disclaim all warranties such as warranties of fitness for a particular purpose. The author or publisher is not liable for any damages whatsoever. The fact that an individual or organization is referred to in this document as a citation or source of information does not imply that the author or publisher endorses the information that the individual or organization provided. This concise summary is unofficial and is not authorized, approved, licensed, or endorsed by the original book's author or publisher.

Table of Contents

Overview 5

Important People 7

Key Takeaways..8

Analysis 11

Key Takeaway 1 11

Key Takeaway 2 13

Key Takeaway 3 15

Key Takeaway 4 17

Key Takeaway 5 18

Key Takeaway 6 19

Key Takeaway 7 20

Key Takeaway 8 22

Key Takeaway 9 24

Key Takeaway 10 25

Key Takeaway 11 26

Key Takeaway 12 27

Author's Style 28

Author's Perspective 30

References 32

Overview

Start With Why by Simon Sinek is a self-help book for business leaders seeking ways of gaining authenticity through a focus on their purpose.

Most companies rely on manipulations to attract customers and employees; they use short-term motivators that do not inspire or encourage loyalty. Customers who are not inspired will stop buying the product as soon as the company cannot keep up the manipulative strategies, and employees are less motivated and less productive when they are not inspired.

Instead of strategies based on keeping up with competitors and metrics meant to determine the company's basic productivity, companies should form strategies that advance its purpose, or its "why," and find metrics that measure "how" the company advances that "why." Only with a firm idea of why the company does its work and how it intends to fulfill that purpose can employees then decide what to do at work. Customers will gravitate toward brands that align with their own purposes, and they will pay a premium in time or cost to buy those products.

Leadership that affirms a company's "why" relies on trust and the cultivation of a culture that ensures that the leader's message is amplified by every employee. This requires a company to forego strategies that seek all possible customers and instead focus on attracting loyal early adopters. It is common for companies to have one inspiring leader who embodies the company's "why" and an energetic leader who can make the plans for the company's "how." The company culture requires consistency through its symbols, such as logos, as well as its strategies.

When a visionary leader leaves, companies tend to lose sight of the focus on "why" and instead focus on shareholder demands or competitive indicators. This loss of focus can also occur at lower levels of the organization as a company becomes large and successful. These lapses can be avoided with consistent metrics, an emphasis on company culture, and a succession plan that perpetuates the leader's vision. Above all, finding and maintaining a company's purpose requires reflection and a struggle to find focus through trial and error.

Start With Why was first published in 2009.

Important People

Simon Sinek is a consultant and public speaker who is an adjunct staff member at the Rand Corporation, where he focuses on military innovation.

Ernest Shackleton (1874-1922) was a British explorer who led pioneering expeditions across the Antarctic.

Wilbur and Orville Wright (1867-1912 and 1871-1948) were inventors who are credited with the first piloted airplane flight.

John Fitzgerald Kennedy (1917-1963) was the 35th president of the United States, known for setting the goal of putting an American astronaut on the moon before 1970.

Martin Luther King Jr. (1929-1968) was a civil rights leader who led marches and boycotts to advocate for racial equality.

Steve Jobs (1955-2011) was the co-founder and chief executive officer of Apple, Inc.

Herb Kelleher is the former CEO of Southwest Airlines.

Gordon Bethune is the former CEO of Continental Airlines. He is widely recognized for rescuing the airline's reputation.

Key Takeaways

1. Current assumptions about business success encourage leaders to focus on competition and manipulating customers to buy, despite evidence that these strategies are ineffective and costly.

2. The best business strategies start with a focus on why the company exists, then on how the company will fulfill that purpose, and lastly on what operations will complete that plan.

3. Customers are attracted to companies whose purposes align with their own because they want to feel a sense of belonging. Those customers will be loyal when a company cannot afford to offer the same low prices or easy access as its competitors.

4. Companies with a focus on their purpose encourage true innovation above and beyond market competition.

5. Statements of why the company exists and how it fulfills that purpose appeal to the limbic brain, which governs emotions. The limbic brain is easier to convince than the neocortex, which recognizes statements of what the company does.

6. Leading a company with a strong sense of purpose involves growing trust, cultivating a

purposeful culture, and seeking employees with a strong sense of purpose who respond well to challenges.

7. Companies are better off building strong relationships with early adopters and courting their loyalty, as opposed to pursuing all potential customers and accepting a low rate of loyalty.

8. Successful companies often have one visionary leader who focuses on "why" and a planning leader who establishes "how." The rest of the organization amplifies the "why" and "how" in what it does.

9. Purpose can be established through consistency in message from leadership, in strategy and practices, and in symbols such as logos.

10. When a visionary leader leaves a company, or when it grows larger, that company can lose its focus on purpose.

11. Ensuring focus on purpose throughout a company's lifetime requires a strong culture and a plan of succession that ensures future leaders maintain the same message.

12. Companies with a strong focus on "why" engage in reflection, learn lessons from failure, and only compete against themselves.

Thank you for purchasing this Instaread book

Download the Instaread mobile app to get unlimited text & audio summaries of bestselling books.

Visit Instaread.co to learn more.

Analysis

Key Takeaway 1

Current assumptions about business success encourage leaders to focus on competition and manipulating customers to buy, despite evidence that these strategies are ineffective and costly.

Analysis

Companies routinely use manipulation to attract customers through pricing, promotions, fear of missed opportunities, desire to emulate others, peer pressure, or novelty. A leading company relies on inspiration and true innovation to attract loyal customers and employees, but most companies are content to use strategies that attract customers in the short term and which are separated from the company's purpose.

A company that exhibited its disinterest in a greater purpose for its product is the manufacturer of EpiPen, a medical device that injects epinephrine to treat an immediate and severe allergic reaction. In August 2016, EpiPen manufacturer Mylan NV was criticized vehemently for raising the wholesale price of its devices from under $50 in 2007 to more than $280 in summer 2016. Because no one else produces EpiPens, the manufacturer could raise prices without concerns about competition. After US politicians urged Mylan to lower those prices, the manufacturer agreed to give coupons for discounts to users whose insurance does not cover the entire cost. However, as with any other coupon program, this plan ensures some customers will pay full price for their purchases because they fail to complete the steps to get a discount or because they don't want to deal with the hassle. [1] If Mylan considered its purpose to be preventing people with life-threatening allergies from dying, raising prices to a point where most current users could not afford to buy the drug would be in opposition to that purpose. Such a move exposes the company as profit-driven rather than purpose-driven, which in turn jeopardizes consumers' trust and loyalty.

Key Takeaway 2

The best business strategies start with a focus on why the company exists, then on how the company will fulfill that purpose, and lastly on what operations will complete that plan.

Analysis

The Golden Circle illustrates where a company should begin its search for strategies. The center of the circle is "why," the company's purpose for existing. The next ring is "how," which relies on an understanding of the purpose and represents the plans to fulfill that purpose. The outer circle, "what," consists of the actions that carry out the plan that fulfills the purpose.

For example, a man who starts with "why" might start by observing a problem insufficiently solved by existing products. He might see the number of people living in areas with poor access to fresh foods, colloquially called food deserts, and decide that the purpose of his new company will be making fresh and healthy food accessible in food deserts at an affordable price. The next step of his company plan is deciding how to fulfill that purpose, which could involve one of a variety of solutions, such as developing a portable grocery store in a truck that brings near-expiration produce from traditional grocery stores into neighborhoods without grocery stores. From this potential "how," the founder and his employees take specific steps to buy trucks, outfit them as mobile grocery stores, build relationships with existing grocery stores to buy produce that would be thrown out, and acquire all the necessary permits. The "how" may be revised as solutions are tried and refined, but the "why" does not change and nothing is done that does not relate to the company's purpose.

Key Takeaway 3

Customers are attracted to companies whose purposes align with their own because they want to feel a sense of belonging. Those customers will be loyal when a company cannot afford to offer the same low prices or easy access as its competitors.

Analysis

If a company has a strong sense of purpose, it will attract customers who feel the same sense of purpose or desire that same purpose in their lives. They voluntarily display the logos of brands that represent that purpose, and they willingly pay premiums of time or money to use products from those brands. Loyal customers will keep buying products from a company with a strong sense of purpose even when the company cannot offer special deals, discounts, or competitive prices.

The need to feel a sense of belonging, and to purchase the products of an identity associated with this sense of belonging, are central concepts in marketing. Brands cultivate customer groups with traits they desire in new customers. They do so in order to ensure that they maintain a particular reputation and identity. A company that tries to change the identity of its brand risks losing customers who view it as a move away from the notion of belonging and purpose they associate with the brand. [2]

This would be especially problematic if the brand includes multiple lines of products associated with that lifestyle identity. For instance, if a brand of kitchenware associates itself with a commitment to culinary culture and to tasteful kitchen decor, the people who purchase that brand's products see themselves as capable and worthy of that identity and recognize it in others when they visit their homes. They will also justify additional expenditure or effort to acquire the brand's products at specialty kitchen stores. Changing the brand's identity to make it more attractive and available to new customers at big-box outlets could be catastrophic to the brand because its customers will no longer trust the presence of the brand's products in someone else's kitchen as an indicator of that person's identity as a chef or homemaker.

In cases like these, it might not necessarily be true that the brand's executives or its employees consider their purpose to be making products with these associations. But a strong sense of purpose for the production of reliable, high-quality products can only improve its customers' opinion of the brand because they will identify more strongly with it.

Key Takeaway 4

Companies with a focus on their purpose encourage true innovation above and beyond market competition.

Analysis

The most innovative businesses are those that fulfill their purposes by offering customers things they later believe they need but did not ask for, such as automobiles and portable music players. A company without a strong sense of "why" would be more likely to only improve existing products and compete with companies offering similar products. Inspiring companies benefit more from measuring how well they fulfill their purpose as innovators.

Someone whose purpose is to innovate within the airline industry might decide to make a faster plane but otherwise fail to impact the transportation sector. This occurred with the development and slow failure of the supersonic Concorde, a line of planes that could break the sound barrier but which were so costly to consumers and airlines that they had to be removed from service. [3] Someone whose greater purpose is to make transportation easier and faster, without worrying about competing with other existing modes of transportation, might instead invent a whole new form of transit. This could happen in the near future with Elon Musk's proposed Hyperloop, which would provide solar-powered, magnetic-propelled rail travel through pressurized tubes. [4]

Key Takeaway 5

Statements of why the company exists and how it fulfills that purpose appeal to the limbic brain, which governs emotions. The limbic brain is easier to convince than the neocortex, which recognizes statements of what the company does.

Analysis

The brain uses two different regions to make decisions. The limbic brain makes what are colloquially called "gut" decisions, which are based on emotion and what just feels right. Customers feel that buying from a company with a familiar sense of purpose is right. Arguments that appeal to the neocortex with numbers or facts do not generate this emotional certainty.

At the same time, businesses that act without a clear sense of purpose can cause distrust because of the limbic response. More than ever, companies must be committed to maintaining the trust of customers and openly communicating with them. This is because many companies rely on continued activity from customers as they shift to subscription models, website memberships, advertising revenue, and advertising that targets past customers. [5] One-time customers are not as useful in these monetization structures as loyal customers, and customers whose guts tell them not to hand over details like email addresses or purchase histories are unlikely to sign up for platforms based on purely logical arguments about financial incentive alone.

Key Takeaway 6

Leading a company with a strong sense of purpose involves growing trust, cultivating a purposeful culture, and seeking employees with a strong sense of purpose who respond well to challenges.

Analysis

Leaders who seek to inspire should work to gain and exhibit trust of employees. They should embody the company's purpose and encourage a culture that specifically values the company's plans to fulfill that purpose. Rather than giving employees metrics to achieve, a leader gives employees challenges and incentives to find solutions.

The history of Nike and its founder, Phil Knight, are clear examples of the success that comes from leaders who direct others with purpose and cultivate trust with employees. Knight's first employees trusted him so much that they left paying jobs to sell the shoes he distributed and did not cash their payroll checks when the company faced difficulties. They took huge risks by starting to produce their own shoes instead of distributing those of a Japanese company and by engaging in new kinds of distribution contracts. Today, Nike is an international brand that dominates the athletic shoe market. Loyal customers proudly display the Nike logo, and Knight continues to lead with the purpose of creating a quality athletic shoe while giving back to society through charitable contributions and mentorship. [6]

Key Takeaway 7

Companies are better off building strong relationships with early adopters and courting their loyalty, as opposed to pursuing all potential customers and accepting a low rate of loyalty.

Analysis

Early adopters make up a minority of consumers, but they are often the most eager to seek out innovation. A company that wants to grow a loyal customer base is better off seeking only customers who fit in the company's culture and share its purpose. Since the average percentage of loyal customers out of all customers including late adopters is closer to 10 percent, a company that focuses on attracting and keeping early adopters to achieve a majority of loyal customers can achieve a higher number of customers that will not abandon the brand.

Changing brand identity to appeal to late adopters can pose difficulties because the new population might not catch on quickly while the early adopters leave for a brand with a consistent message. This is one challenge currently faced by Coach, a luxury bag brand seeking a higher-income customer base with its creation of a line of coats and accessories. Coach is simultaneously eliminating the many sales, discounts, and coupons that allowed its original customer base, the middle market of the luxury brand industry, to afford Coach's products. This decision was likely intended to secure Coach's reputation as a luxury brand that can afford to charge high prices, but without its loyal customers involved, the transition has not been smooth. [7]

Key Takeaway 8

Successful companies often have one visionary leader who focuses on "why" and a planning leader who establishes "how." The rest of the organization amplifies the "why" and "how" in what it does.

Analysis

Leaders often come in pairs, one of whom inspires employees and customers with vision while the other uses energy to drive the pursuit of that vision with a plan. If the message from the "why" and "how" leaders is consistent and matches the purpose of the employees, they will amplify those messages to each other and to the customers.

The employees at Facebook, as represented by Antonio Martinez in his memoir *Chaos Monkeys* (2016), fit into this framework of a business run by an inspired leader, Mark Zuckerberg. In Martinez's view, Zuckerberg is a visionary with big goals who has left the practices and strategies up to other top employees, such as "star" COO Sheryl Sandberg, as long as they fit the company's culture. That culture involves long hours worked by people passionate about the product's ability to connect people, share information, and improve services that rely on Facebook. Employees maintained that culture by ensuring that Zuckerberg's activities and those of his executives were transparent. They maintained that company culture by holding company-wide meetings to ensure that everyone received the same message and creating working spaces that were laden with symbols of their mission to connect the world. [8]

Key Takeaway 9

Purpose can be established through consistency in message from leadership, in strategy and practices, and in symbols such as logos.

Analysis

A company's message is only clear if its strategies, practices, and culture are consistent with its purpose. This extends to symbols used by the company including logos, which are often generic or represent nothing in particular.

This consistency through symbols and leadership is apparent in designs for Olympic logos. The graphic design of every Olympic games is subject to enormous scrutiny because of its symbolic importance. Each logo is expected to represent a country or city as well as the spirit of fair competition in the games. Some of these designs have been well-meaning but unclear, while others conveyed motion or harmony, or were designed specifically for the screens or T-shirts on which they would be displayed. The host country often chooses a design by holding a contest to find the best entry through public vote. [9]

Key Takeaway 10

When a visionary leader leaves a company, or when it grows larger, that company can lose its focus on purpose.

Analysis

Even companies that begin with a strong sense of purpose can lose that vision. When the metrics change from measuring the pursuit of the purpose to the pursuit of market share or profit margins, loyal customers leave and employees cease to receive and relay the company's message clearly.

The nature of publicly owned companies means that shareholders are always an especially difficult factor to measure and manage when attempting to maintain a focus on purpose. Shareholders are not chosen by company creators or executives, unless they plan ahead and retain control or create different classes of stock. A significant shareholder who decides to get involved for reasons unaligned with the company's purpose can exert pressure on executives to meet metrics of market competition. If shareholders become too focused on competition, profit margins, or market share, they might not have the patience to understand why purpose is more important. Shareholders can vote to replace some executives if those demands are not met, and they might choose new candidates who place high importance on profits or market share at the continued expense of the company's purpose.

Key Takeaway 11

Ensuring focus on purpose throughout a company's lifetime requires a strong culture and a plan of succession that ensures future leaders maintain the same message.

Analysis

A company with a culture that amplifies the message all the way to the lowest-ranked employees, and which seeks leaders who want to pursue the original purpose, can survive scaling up or replacing leaders because everyone keeps the purpose and plan in mind.

Researchers looking at organizations with a uniquely developmental approach suggest ways to do this with functional feedback and goal-setting systems that go all the way up and down the corporate structure. Some organizations provide company-wide transparent criticism and recommendation systems. Others use mentorship programs, company-wide meetings, and programs for setting goals and receiving advice on how to achieve those goals, for everyone from the newest employees to the executives. The most important thing is that these systems are custom-made for each company, support its purpose, and apply equally to all employees. [10]

Key Takeaway 12

Companies with a strong focus on "why" engage in reflection, learn lessons from failure, and only compete against themselves.

Analysis

In order for a company to find its purpose, it must look back at the original inspiration and the lessons learned from failed efforts to compete or retain customers. A company with a clear sense of purpose does not need to measure how it competes against others. Instead, it works to improve itself and uses those measures of improvement to attract customers.

Companies will sometimes pursue their purpose by removing themselves from competition. In 2014, the CVS chain of pharmacies decided to stop selling cigarettes because it was inconsistent with their goal of providing health care to customers. CVS also increased the prescription co-pay for customers using its prescription-filling service at retail outlets that continued to sell tobacco products. Analysts estimated these decisions would reduce CVS's revenue by $2 billion that year alone. [11] Such a move may have been a considerable sacrifice for a branding benefit, but doing so ensured that customers saw CVS practicing its purpose at its own expense. The year that CVS stopped selling tobacco products, sales increased by more than $12 billion over 2013 sales, and its sales continued to rise through 2015. [12]

Author's Style

Simon Sinek writes in the style of a lecture or presentation referring to the readership as "many of you," or similar phrases aimed at an assumed audience. The writing is lively and moves quickly from example to lesson to advice. Sinek peppers the narrative with platitudes, such as when he states that there is a difference between leaders and those who lead.

Sinek draws examples from history, many of which are common examples of innovation or paradigm shifts. He cites the development of theories of the round Earth and the Wright brothers' first flight, but without contributing any new perspectives. He uses few originally researched examples to illustrate his points. Some of these examples are reused in later chapters in similar form to their first appearance in earlier chapters.

Some examples and illustrations for concepts come from Sinek's life, both from his work as a consultant for business leaders and from his personal venture to write a book. Sinek identifies specific companies by name as negative examples and frequently uses a few companies as positive examples, namely Apple, Inc., SouthWest Airlines, and Harley-Davidson.

Sinek uses some existing words in unique ways. When "why," "how," and "what" are used as nouns, they are written in all-capital letters. He also coins the concentric circle diagram of these three notions as "the Golden Circle," in reference to the Golden Ratio in geometry, and coins other terms directly related to applications of why, how, and what.

Some concepts are illustrated with diagrams that are useful visual ways of remembering them. Sources of quotes and statistics are cited at the end of the book, marked with page numbers and divided by chapter, but the narrative itself contains no superscripts or links to tell the reader that sources are listed elsewhere.

Author's Perspective

Simon Sinek is employed by the Rand Corporation. He is also a consultant and public speaker. He originally planned to become a lawyer but left law school to pursue the goal of inspiring others to pursue their goals. His inspirations include self-help classics such as *The 7 Habits of Highly Effective People* (1989) by Stephen Covey and *Who Moved My Cheese?* (1998) by Spencer Johnson, as well as behavioral economics authors Malcolm Gladwell, Steven Levitt, Stephen Dubner, and Nicholas Taleb, and finally, psychoanalyst Viktor Frankl. He gained popularity following a series of talks for TED conferences sponsored independently and by the Sapling Foundation.

~~~~ END OF INSTAREAD ~~~~

Thank you for purchasing this Instaread book

Download the Instaread mobile app to get unlimited text & audio summaries of bestselling books.

Visit Instaread.co to learn more.

References

1. Kodjak, Alison. "EpiPen Manufacturer Says It Will Help With Out-Of-Pocket Costs." *NPR Shots Blog*. August 24, 2016. Accessed August 27, 2016. http://www.npr.org/sections/health-shots/2016/08/24/491232665/latest-target-in-the-drug-price-wars-the-ubiquitous-epipen

2. Berger, Jonah. *Invisible Influence: The Hidden Forces That Shape Behavior*. New York: Simon & Schuster, 2016.

3. Westcott, Richard. "Could Concorde ever fly again? No, says British Airways." *BBC News*. October 24, 2013. Accessed August 27, 2016. http://www.bbc.com/news/business-24629451

4. Nicol, Will. "As Hyperloop Progress Glides Forward, Here's What You Need to Know." *Digital Trends*. February 3, 2016. Accessed August 27, 2016. http://www.digitaltrends.com/cool-tech/hyperloop-news/

5. Choudary, Sangeet, et al. *Platform Revolution: How Networked Markets Are Transforming the Economy—And How to Make Them Work for You*. New York: W.W. Norton & Company, 2016.

6. Knight, Phil. *Shoe Dog*. New York: Scribner, 2016.

7. Enaje, Melissa. "Coach Inc.'s bid to revitalize its brand isn't in the bag." *Medill Reports Chicago*.

November 5, 2014. Accessed September 8, 2016. https://medillreports.com/2014/11/05/coach-inc-s-bid-to-revitalize-its-brand-isnt-in-the-bag/

8. Martinez, Antonio. *Chaos Monkeys: Obscene Fortune and Random Failure in Silicon Valley*. New York: Harper, 2016.

9. Brillon, James. "The best and worst Olympic logo designs since 1924." *Dezeen Magazine*. August 8, 2016. Accessed August 27, 2016. http://www.dezeen.com/2016/08/08/olympic-games-logo-designs-london-rio-tokyo/

10. Kegan, Robert, et al. *An Everyone Culture: Becoming a Deliberately Developmental Organization*. Boston: Harvard Business Review Press, 2016.

11. Marino, Jonathan. "How CVS turned its cigarette ban into a strategic weapon." *Business Insider*. February 12, 2015. Accessed August 27, 2016. http://www.businessinsider.com/rite-aid-buys-pbm-to-avoid-getting-smoked-by-the-competition-2015-2

12. Pearson, Bryan. "When The Butt Stopped Here: What Banning Tobacco has Meant for CVS." *Forbes*. September 3, 2015. Accessed September 8, 2016. http://www.forbes.com/sites/bryanpearson/2015/09/03/when-the-butt-stopped-here-what-banning-tobacco-has-meant-for-cvs/#6a8b910e2e9b

Lightning Source UK Ltd.
Milton Keynes UK
UKHW010940080319
338731UK00013B/490/P